PROFILES · IN · MUSIC

LIBRARY OF CONGRESS CATALOGING-IN-PUBLICATION DATA

Loewen, Nancy, 1964-
    James Brown / by Nancy Loewen.
      p. cm. -- (Profiles in music)
    Includes index.
    Summary: A biography of the popular singer, dancer, and
songwriter who earned the nickname "Godfather of Soul."
    ISBN 0-86592-607-7
    1. Brown, James, 1928- --Juvenile literature. 2. Soul
musicians--United States--Biography--Juvenile literature.
[1. Brown, James, 1928- . 2. Musicians. 3. Soul music.
4. Afro-Americans--Biography.] I. Title. II. Series: Loewen,
Nancy, 1964- Profiles in music.
ML3930.B87L6 1989
782.42164'4'092--dc20
[B]   89-32265
                                         CIP
                                    AC MN

© **1989 Rourke Enterprises, Inc.**

PROFILES · IN · MUSIC

James Brown

TEXT BY
NANCY LOEWEN

DESIGN & PRODUCTION BY
MARK E. AHLSTROM
(The Bookworks)

1964

ROURKE
ENTERPRISES,
INC.
Vero Beach, FL 32964
U.S.A.

JAMES BROWN
1933-

TABLE
OF
CONTENTS

CREDITS

Frank Christian Studio/Universal Attractions:
cover photo, page 4

All other photos:
The Michael Ochs Archives
Venice, California

(Special credit:
Paulsen/Michael Ochs Archives, page 60)

TYPESETTING AND LAYOUT: THE FINAL WORD
PRINTING: WORZALLA PUBLISHING CO.

James Brown: Soul Brother Number One

It is April 5, 1968, and there is trouble in the United States. Just one day earlier, civil rights leader Martin Luther King, Jr., was assassinated in Memphis while showing his support for striking garbage workers. King had been loved by millions of people. Now that he is dead, people of all races are angry and afraid. Riots are breaking out in many large cities all across the country. The nation is on edge.

In Boston, public officials are hoping desperately to avoid the violence that is occurring in other cities. They have a plan—a risky one, but one that might just keep people off the streets. Soul singer James Brown had been scheduled to give a concert at the Boston Garden Arena. Now, despite the tragedy of Dr. King's death, it has been decided that the concert will go on as planned. Not only that, but the performance will also be broadcast on local television. Boston Mayor Kevin White and other city leaders are praying that the show will help calm people. James Brown is a hero to much of the black community, and to other·people as well. Maybe the citizens of Boston will listen to him instead of taking their anger to the streets. Maybe Boston will escape the destruction that is already happening across the nation.

It will be hard for James Brown to concentrate on his music tonight. He considers Dr. King a friend—to himself and to all of America. But he knows that tonight, his people need to hear his music. They need to be reminded of the strength they still possess.

The show begins. James Brown steps up to the microphone. "Let's not do anything to dishonor Dr. King," he says to the televison cameras and to the troubled audience in front of him. "Stay home. You kids, especially, I want you to think about what you're doing. Think about what Dr. King stood for. Don't just react in a way that's going to destroy your community."

With that he starts singing in the raw, soulful style that has made him one of the top-selling artists of all time. Between songs he talks some more to his audience, both in their homes and in the arena. Through his words and his music, James Brown helps people deal with their grief. He lets them know that even though a great leader is dead, the dream of a better future is still within their grasp.

While all of this is happening, officials are keeping a close watch on the city. The concert is having a tremendous effect, it seems. In some areas, the streets are nearly empty! Someone suggests that the concert be broadcast again, right after the first showing is over. Brown agrees. By the time the second concert is off the air, it's two o'clock in the morning.

Thanks to James Brown, Boston got through that terrible night with very little trouble.

• • •

James Brown, along with others such as Ray Charles and Sam Cooke, is one of the pioneers of soul music. This type of music became popular in the early 1960's. It combines elements of gospel with rhythm and blues (often referred to as R & B). Sometimes it discusses social issues, such as Brown's "Say it Loud, I'm Black and I'm Proud." More often, the theme is love or romantic relationships. But the lyrics are usually not as important as the rhythms and the way the music makes people feel. One musician described soul as "the part of playing you can't get out of books or studies."

For more than 30 years, attending a James Brown concert has been an out-of-the-ordinary experience. It all starts with emcee Danny Ray announcing dramatically, "Ladies and gentlemen, it's star time!" As the crowds stir in excitement, he shouts out the names of Brown's many hit songs. Then he lists Brown's latest titles—"Godfather of Soul! The Hardest Working Man in Show Business! Mr. Dynamite!" By the time "The Legend of Soul Himself" takes the stage, the crowds seem ready to explode.

Onstage, James Brown makes use of horns, guitars, and drums to add depth and flair to his music. But his most compelling instrument is his voice. As Brown sings, he also grunts, screeches, and groans. He dazzles people with his stylish costumes. Then he dances so hard—splits, jumps, kneedrops—that he is bathed in sweat by the end of a show. Audiences join in with handclapping and shouts.

Brown's music has been described as being "on a wavelength direct to the gut." Listeners either love it or hate it, but they always react. And that's just the way James Brown wants it. Throughout his long career, he has never tamed down his intense style in order to be more commercial. Yet his records have sold by the millions, and his concerts have usually sold out.

Brown's list of honors is almost as long as his list of nicknames. Early in his career, he had 17 hits in a time span of just two years. In 1986, he won a Grammy Award for the song, "Living in America." He was one of the first musicians to be inducted into the Rock and Roll Hall of Fame. And with 114 charted singles, he is considered the most popular black musician of all time.

To his many fans, James Brown really is Soul Brother Number One.

James Brown—"The Legend of Soul"—is perhaps the most popular black musician of all time.

Througout his career, James Brown has been known for his dancing and stage moves. Growing up poor in Augusta, Georgia, he used to dance for World War II soldiers, who often threw him their spare change.

CHAPTER 1 — AN UNUSUAL CHILDHOOD

*"It gave me my own mind. No matter
what came my way after that, I had
the ability to fall back on myself."*

—James Brown on his early
childhood, spent in the woods

Boy in the Woods

James Brown was born on May 3, 1933. That was during the Great Depression, a time when jobs were scarce and the U.S. economy was bad. For black people, the times were especially hard. Segregation and discrimination were common then. There were few opportunities for them to get good educations, or to get jobs that paid well.

James Brown's parents, Joe and Susie, lived in a cabin in the woods near Barnwell, South Carolina. That cabin is where Brown was born. Two aunts came over to help with the birth. At first, everyone thought the baby was stillborn. Then Aunt Minnie took matters into her own hands. She patted the baby and breathed into his tiny mouth. Suddenly the baby gave out a piercing cry. James Brown was alive and well, after all!

While Susie took care of the baby, Joe worked as hard as he could—at whatever job he could find. Sometimes he worked on a farm or on a construction crew. Other times he worked at a gas station.

Although he was an excellent heavy equipment operator, he couldn't pass the test to get certified. He only had a second-grade education.

When James Brown was just four years old, his parents split up. "That's one of my earliest memories," Brown related in his autobiography, *Godfather of Soul*. "My mother was standing in the door of the cabin getting ready to leave, and my father was facing her." Susie knew that Joe would probably be able to support their son better than she could. She told her husband to keep the child. With that, she walked out the door. It would be 20 years before mother and son would see each other again.

After Susie left, James Brown and his father moved from one shack in the woods to another. The shacks didn't have electricity or running water. Most of them weren't even painted. Because Joe was always working, the young James Brown spent a lot of time alone in the woods. Sometimes, when Joe was working far away, he was even alone at night. It could get pretty scary for such a small boy!

Still, all that time by himself probably helped

James Brown become what he is today. "It gave me my own mind," Brown has said. "No matter what came my way after that, I had the ability to fall back on myself."

When James Brown was five years old, his father came home with a surprise present. "Hey, son, what do you think of this?" Joe said, and started playing a tune on a 10-cent harmonica. James Brown quickly learned to play the small instrument. The harmonica was like a friend to him. Playing it made him feel less alone.

944 Twiggs Street

Although Joe Brown did his best to take care of his young son, he knew that James needed someone who would be around more. He realized that his son should not be alone as he was growing up. Finally, he convinced Aunt Minnie to come and live with them. At that time they were living near Robbins, South Carolina.

A short time later, Joe Brown decided he could

probably make more money in Augusta, Georgia. The family moved, but didn't stay together. Aunt Minnie took James to live with another aunt, who had a house in Augusta. Joe found work in the area, and visited his son as often as he could.

James Brown's new address was 944 Twiggs Street. This was no ordinary place for a young child to live. It was a house of gambling, moonshine, and prostitution. There were always a lot of people hanging around. Aunt Honey managed the household. She was a smart woman, and a warmhearted one, too. Though much of what she did was illegal, Honey was just trying to survive, like a lot of other people.

Every few months, Honey would get busted by the police for her activities. But she was never in jail very long, and as soon as she'd get back, it was business as usual. At other times she was able to avoid going to jail at all. A few words—or a little money—to the right person could often take care of the problem.

Honey—whose real name was Handsome Washington—was a very generous person. Men who were out of work often stayed at her house until they could line up some employment. Aunt Honey always made sure that everyone had enough to eat. She often gave money to the young mothers living in the alley behind the house. She couldn't stand the thought of them not having money to buy groceries for their children.

James Brown's father was now working in a furniture store. One day the owners let him have an old pump organ that was missing a leg. Though the organ was useless to the store owners, Joe knew just what to do with it! He put the organ on the porch at the Twiggs Street house, carefully propping up one corner with a cheese crate.

That night, Joe came by the house after work. The porch was crowded with people. Joe's heart skipped a beat. Maybe there had been an accident, or a fight! He ran up to the house and squeezed through the crowd. There, sitting at the broken organ, was his son. In just one day, James Brown had taught himself how to work the instrument. Now he was picking out a song everyone knew, smiling happily.

After that, Honey paid more attention to her nephew. One day Aunt Honey was giving Brown a bath. She looked at the pattern of wet hair on his arm. "Look at this!" she said, holding out his arm. "It's a sign. You're going to be very rich someday!" Brown laughed at her. He couldn't even imagine such a thing. But Honey just nodded wisely. She repeated her prediction whenever she gave him a bath. Each time, James Brown just laughed as if it was the funniest thing he'd ever heard.

Spare Change

Around that time, everyone was talking about the war that was taking place in Europe—World War II. America was not yet in the war. But by 1940, more and more servicemen from nearby Fort Gordon were coming into Augusta. Seven-year-old James Brown was too young to understand much about the war. All he knew was that the more soldiers there were, the greater the chances of making money at Twiggs Street.

Honey had a grandson named Willie Glenn who also lived at the house. Willie was just a year older than James. Everyone called him Big Junior, and Brown, in turn, was called Little Junior. The two boys had a lot of fun together. They were like brothers.

Right by their house was the Third Level Canal Bridge. Soldiers were always passing over the bridge in their long lines of trucks. The traffic was often slowed to a crawl—and the two boys made the most of these times. While Big Junior patted out a beat, James Brown would do a country dance for the soldiers. If they liked the little show, they would throw their spare change to the boys. Usually it was just pennies, nickels, and dimes. Sometimes, though, a soldier would throw down a big, heavy quarter. Just the thought of those quarters kept the two boys working hard!

As much as they wanted to keep the money for themselves, they usually turned it over to Honey to help her pay the rent on the house. Rent was just five dollars a month. But even with all the people staying there, the family had a hard time getting it together some months. When there was enough money to pay the rent for the month, though, the boys spent what was left on movies or food.

By now, James Brown was attending Floyd School, one of the few black schools in Augusta. He was a small kid, but soon got a reputation for being tough. For some reason, his classmates called him "Jamesbrown," as if his name was all one word.

For Brown, the worst part about school was that he didn't have nice clothes to wear. Sometimes the principal would even send him home because of it! That made him feel terrible. A friend of his father's helped him out now and then by getting new clothes for him. Then school would go smoothly for a while. But it didn't take long before the new clothes were worn out or too small. Then the whole situation was repeated.

After school, James Brown and Big Junior had lots of things to do. Besides dancing for the soldiers, they shined shoes, delivered groceries, and picked cotton and peanuts. Music was an important part of their lives, too. James, Big Junior, and their friends would often get together to sing gospel songs. Some neighbors taught James Brown to play the guitar and piano, which added to the fun.

The war was still going on. It seemed like there were more soldiers in Augusta every year. And hundreds of German prisoners were being held at the Augusta Arsenal. During the day the prisoners did farmwork and other jobs. That meant there was less work available for people like Joe Brown.

Things were changing on another front as well. The raids at Honey's house were happening more often. And it was taking longer for her to be released from jail. One day, after giving James something to eat, she said in a troubled voice, "We've got to move." Brown knew that something bad must have happened, but he couldn't guess what it could be. He just went along with the move.

Now the family separated once more. Aunt Minnie and James Brown moved to a two-room shack and lived by themselves. Joe Brown still came by to visit, but it seemed like he wasn't around as often as he had been before. All of these changes were upsetting to Brown. "When you're a kid your home is home, even if it's a roadhouse," he wrote in his autobiography. "I was sorry to see it broken up."

James Brown won a talent contest when he was 11 years old. He's been thrilling audiences ever since!

*While serving time for theft at the age of 16, James Brown
was nicknamed "Music Box" by his fellow inmates.*

2 CHAPTER | A WRONG TURN

"I know I don't have any education, but I can sing. And I want to get out and sing for the Lord."

—James Brown writing to his parole board

Music
and Sports

James Brown had never been able to spend much time with his father, and for a time he wasn't able to see his father at all. Joe Brown had joined the U.S. Navy, partly because he couldn't find a good job. Once in the navy, however, he sent home what money he could to Aunt Minnie. This money went toward paying the rent and buying food. If they needed anything else, James Brown would have to shine shoes or dance for the soldiers to earn the money for it.

Music of all kinds was always around, whether on the radio or just about the town. Brown listened carefully to all the newest sounds. Then he'd try to play the songs on whatever instrument was handy. He'd sing, too, imitating the different styles of popular singers.

Brown's interest in music started paying off when he was 11 years old. The Lenox Theater, a movie house, held an amateur talent contest. Just for the fun of it, James Brown decided to enter. He sang "So Long"—and his voice was so strong and soulful that he won first prize!

The next year he formed his first band with some of his friends. They called themselves the "Cremona Trio." The boys didn't have any instruments of their own. They had to borrow instruments from the school, or from whomever had them. James Brown usually played the piano and sang. Sometimes he played the drums.

Occasionally the Cremona Trio was invited to perform at local schools. During these times, James Brown realized that he did indeed have a talent for singing. Not only did he have a powerful voice—he could sing all night if he had to!

As much fun as he was having with the Cremona Trio, James Brown wasn't thinking about a career in music—yet. He was good at sports, and, like many kids, dreamed about becoming a professional athlete.

One of his interests was baseball. The famous Ty Cobb had lived in Augusta, and Brown knew all about him. Besides that, the Detroit Tigers had a minor league team in Augusta, and held their spring training there as well. James Brown thought he'd make a pretty good left-handed pitcher.

Football was another one of Brown's favorite sports. Once he broke his leg during a game. But that didn't keep James Brown away from football for long. Somehow he convinced the coach that he could still play. He just went ahead and played, wearing his cast. Later he broke the same leg again, and did the same thing—played with a cast. It's no wonder James Brown had a reputation for being a tough kid!

Baseball and football were fun, but in Brown's eyes, no sport could compare to boxing. That's what he really wanted to do. He practiced his punches at a black community center, as well as in the schoolyard and in the streets. Brown's idol was Beau Jack, a lightweight world champion who was from Augusta, too. In fact, Beau Jack had even shined shoes in the same places James Brown had.

It's No Game

In 1945 the war was finally over. Joe Brown came back to Augusta. It was a tough time, though. The servicemen—and all the money they had brought into the town—were gone. Jobs were scarce, and food prices shot up for a time because of shortages. Once again, Joe worked at whatever job he could find. Often, though, he lost his money at gambling.

Around this time James Brown began to steal. It started as a way to get some decent clothes for school. Since neither his father nor Aunt Minnie had much money, he figured he'd have to take care of himself.

Eventually James Brown joined a small gang. Most of the gangs then weren't as violent as they are today. Mostly the young men just hung out together. But sometimes they stole, too. At first they just swiped stuff from open porches. Then, gradually, the stealing became more serious. Brown and his friends would break into cars and take whatever was inside. They also took hubcaps, gas caps, and batteries. Then they sold the stuff for the highest price they could get.

Brown did set some limits for himself when it came to stealing. He never stole from a black person, because so many of them were poor, too. And he never forgot his friends. One time he stole a whole bunch of baseball gloves—a real luxury— and passed them out to the guys. Whenever he could, he'd help out the other kids who didn't have nice clothes to wear to school. "I didn't think twice about stealing them a jacket, or a shirt, or a pair of pants," said James Brown in *Godfather of Soul.*

Big Junior didn't like what was happening to his friend. "You're going to get caught sooner or later," he kept telling Brown. "I don't want to go to jail, and I don't want you to go to jail either!" But James Brown just laughed. He was so quick and sure of himself, he couldn't imagine anyone ever catching him. That soon happened, however.

One night James Brown and some other guys were hard at work, disconnecting a car battery. They were so involved in what they were doing that they didn't notice the policemen standing behind them. The cops had to tap them on the shoulder to get their attention!

The boys were all sent to the Richmond County Jail, where they had to stay overnight. A juvenile officer gave them a stern lecture the next morning. Then they were released. "You see?" Big Junior said. "I told you this would happen!" But James Brown hardly listened. As soon as he was released, he went right back to his old habits. For James Brown, and a lot of other poor kids, stealing had become a way of life.

It wasn't long before Brown was caught again. This time he made the police work a little harder to catch him. When they couldn't get to him on foot, they chased him in their squad cars, in and out of alleys. Brown ran as fast as he could. He was sure that he'd lose them eventually. But then he ducked into a dead-end alley, and that was the end of the chase.

James Brown was fingerprinted. A mug shot was taken. All of this was very frightening to him, but when the police detectives questioned him, he didn't try to hide anything. Brown was charged with four counts of breaking and entering and theft from an automobile. Even though he was only 15 years old, James Brown was thrown in with the adult offenders.

Four months passed. Nobody said anything to him about bail or lawyers. He spent most of his time on his bunk, thinking and daydreaming. It reminded him of all the time he spent alone in the woods when he was young. On Sundays, Big Junior would come to visit him, usually bringing a special treat—chewing gum. The rest of his family, however, rarely visited. "It would break my heart to see him in jail," Aunt Honey declared.

James Brown's 16th birthday came and went, and he still didn't know what would happen to him. Then, on June 13, 1949, he got his answer. A widely publicized bribery case was scheduled to be tried that day. The courthouse was packed with onlookers, mostly white people. When the trial was delayed, officials decided to try some of their other cases instead. One of these cases was James Brown's. He was to be tried as an adult—even though he was only in the seventh grade.

Brown's heart sank when he heard the words "eight to sixteen years." That was the maximum sentence for the crimes he had committed.

Big Junior had been right. This was no game. This was real.

Music Box

James Brown was ordered to serve his sentence in the Georgia Juvenile Training Institute in Rome, Georgia. One Sunday afternoon before he was to be moved to Rome, Big Junior came to visit him. He looked so discouraged that Brown wanted to cheer him up. "Don't worry, Junior," he said suddenly. "When I get out of here the **world** is going to know about me." Big Junior just shook his head. He thought cell life was making his friend crazy.

When James Brown was transferred to the center in Rome, his days became very predictable. He was up every morning by six o'clock. After breakfast, everyone went to work. Some days Brown worked on a nearby farm or helped build houses. Other times he worked in the prison kitchen or laundry. Lunch was from noon to one, and then the prisoners went back to their jobs. Quitting time was at 4:30.

After supper, the inmates had some time to themselves. They played baseball or football if there was enough light. Later they'd go inside and play dominoes or cards. What James Brown liked most, though, was listening to music. A friend named Johnny Terry had a radio. He let Brown listen to it whenever he wanted.

One night when he was fiddling with the radio, some music caught his ear. He turned the knob back a little to get the sound more clearly. Sure enough, that was R & B! He got so excited that he lost his grip on the radio. It crashed onto the floor and broke into what seemed like a million pieces.

Brown felt horrible. Trying to make it up to his friend, he got some wire and tape and started putting the radio back together. When he was done, the radio looked like a pile of junk. Amazingly, though, it still worked!

After James Brown had been in the correctional facility for a couple of months, he found a new way to pass the time. With Johnny Terry and two other friends nicknamed Shag and Huckle-buck, he formed a gospel quartet. Singing the old songs helped them feel content.

The quartet practiced most evenings. They kept improving, and before long everyone thought they sounded pretty good. Once a guard even took them to sing for people in a nearby hospital. The four young men sang so well that they brought tears to the patients' eyes.

After a while, the group added some home-made instruments to their act. They used empty lard cans as drums, and made a mandolin out of a wooden box. All this time, though, they had their eye on the piano in the prison gym. Finally the officials let them use it. During half-time at prison basketball games, James Brown sang and accompanied himself on the piano. The guys started calling him "Music Box."

"All I Want is a Chance"

After James Brown had been in prison for two years, the Juvenile Training Institute was moved to an area near Toccoa, Georgia. Brown kept up with his music and sports in the new location. Sometimes the inmates went into town and played the high school sports teams. They were so strong from all their hard work that they usually won. And if there was a piano in the gym, James Brown would soon gather a crowd after the game.

Now and then the kids from town would go out to the prison and hang around by the fence. They thought it was fun to watch the "jailbirds." The prisoners weren't really bothered by this. They liked talking with the town kids through the fence.

One day Brown got to talking music with a tall, skinny kid from town. His name was Bobby Byrd, and he had put together a gospel group, too. The two young musicians talked for a long time. Later on, it was Bobby Byrd and his group that gave James Brown his first chance at success.

When Brown turned 19, he started doing some serious thinking. His long sentence just didn't make any sense to him. Finally he decided to write a letter to his parole board. It might not do any good, but it was sure worth a try. He realized that his life was just wasting away.

"I'm like any other person," James Brown wrote. "All I want is a chance." Then he added, "I know I don't have any education, but I can sing. And I want to get out and sing for the Lord."

The parole board was impressed. They told James Brown he could leave, under two conditions: he had to have a job, and he had to stay in Toccoa. Brown was delighted, but a little confused. Why couldn't he go back to Augusta, where his father and Aunt Minnie were living? And how could he get a job if he couldn't go out and look for one? It might be a long time before he could leave the prison!

James Brown was lucky. The very next Saturday he was out in a field, loading rocks into a truck. A man was watching him, and the two started talking. It turned out that the man owned an automobile dealership in Toccoa. "I'll give you a job," the man said when he found out the condition of Brown's parole.

James Brown was able to leave the institute that same day. It was June 14, 1952—just over three years since he'd been convicted.

CHAPTER 3

A TASTE OF SUCCESS

"I want you to record for King Records."

—Ralph Bass, talent scout for King

A Different Direction

When James Brown was released from prison, his interests stayed the same. He still spent most of his time with sports and music. Outside of the prison walls, though, everything seemed a lot more fun.

One condition of Brown's parole was that he find a stable place to live. At first he stayed with Bobby Byrd's family. But their house was already crowded, and they couldn't take on another person for very long. Finally he moved in with a couple called Dora and Nathaniel Davis, who ran a barbershop. They treated James Brown like a son.

With the Davises, Brown started attending the Trinity CME Church. He joined their church choir, as well as a gospel group called the Community Choir. The Community Choir gave programs in churches and schools. Sometimes they were even featured on the local radio station.

Bobby Byrd still had his gospel group together. He kept asking James Brown to join the group, too.

But Brown was just too busy to accept the offer. During the day he worked at Lawson Motors, washing and greasing cars. Most of his spare time was taken up by the Community Choir and his church choir. And then there was baseball. He had to squeeze in enough time for that, too!

Unfortunately, James Brown soon lost his job. One of his bosses was always trying to push him around. Brown hated it, but he tried to hold his temper. One day Brown had just finished washing and waxing a nice 1950 Ford. "Do it again," his boss growled for no apparent reason.

Brown was angry, so he decided to take the car for a spin. If he had to wash it all over again, he might as well get it a little dusty, right? But getting dusty wasn't all that happened to the car. Brown hadn't done that much driving. He took a turn too fast and ended up in the ditch. When he drove the car back into the lot, with one wheel wobbling crazily, he knew right away he was in trouble. He was fired on the spot.

At first the parole officer threatened to send James Brown back to prison. But Bobby Byrd's mother put in a good word for Brown. And when Brown got a new job right away—in a plastics factory—the matter was dropped.

The threat of having to return to prison had a big effect on Brown. He started thinking more about what he wanted to do with his life. He loved singing in the choirs, but they weren't performing that much anymore. Besides, he was ready to do a little experimenting with his music. The next time Bobby Byrd asked him to join his group, James Brown said he would.

The Flames

Besides Brown and Byrd, there were six other young men in the group. One of them was Johnny Terry, who had just been released from prison. Though the group had been rather informal up to this point, they now started working a little harder. The group practiced whenever they could, usually at the Byrd home. The only instrument they had was an old piano.

At first they didn't sound that great, either.

Their voices didn't seem to blend very well, and they couldn't decide what kind of music to sing. But after they'd been practicing awhile, things started coming together. They decided to copy the style of rhythm and blues artists like Billy Ward and the Dominoes, the Orioles, and the Five Royales. Even without instruments, they sounded pretty good. James Brown also kept up with the latest dances, including the slop, the funky chicken, the alligator, and the camel walk.

Now came the next step—performing for real. Their first gig was at Bill's Rendezvous Club in Toccoa. The club was owned by Bill and Delois Keith. They were neighbors of the Davises, Brown's sponsor family. The group started playing the club once or twice a week.

Even though their only instrument was the club's piano, the singers impressed people with their energy. They made up for their lack of instruments by doing other things. They stomped their feet to keep time. And no matter what, they never stopped singing. Looking back at that period, Brown has said, "We learned to make a whole lot of noise with very few resources. I think that's eventually what made us so powerful and gave me the stamina to sing and dance like I do."

The group started playing other gigs in the area. But even though they were becoming popular, they still didn't have a name. They'd started out as the Avons, but had to drop the name when they found out another group was using it. Eventually the decision was made for them. People just started calling them the Toccoa Band, and the name stuck—for a while at least.

One of the group members had a brother who knew how to play the guitar. To get him to join the group, they offered him a little "bribe." With everyone chipping in, they bought an electric guitar and a small amplifier. The guitar added some needed excitement to their act. Before long they were playing so many gigs that they hired a manager, an undertaker named Barry Trimier.

Most of the gigs were at night. Sometimes, though, they had daytime performances. They often played during the intermissions of intramural basketball games at a local white high school.

The kids loved the Toccoa Band. One time Brown came sliding and dancing onto the gym floor with a big dust mop, and the kids went crazy.

The daytime gigs were fun, but a little risky, too. Most members of the group had jobs. They had to sneak away whenever they had a show to do. Because James Brown's job was a condition of his parole, this situation made him a little nervous. Still, nothing could keep him from performing.

James Brown was determined to play music and keep his job. He was also determined to do something else—get married. For some time he'd been bringing a young woman named Velma Warren to the shows. Actually, having Velma there made him even more popular. The guys in the crowd then knew that Brown wasn't after their girlfriends!

On June 19, 1953, the couple was married at the Trinity Church in Toccoa. "I wanted a real home and a steady family, which I had never really had before," James Brown explained in *Godfather of Soul*. "That was what I saw myself working for, whether as a singer or as a laborer—to be able to establish a home."

Around this time, though, there were problems within the band. Without really intending to, James Brown had become the main performer. He sang the lead songs and did the solo dances. Bobby Byrd was in the spotlight a lot, too. Some of the other members were jealous. They started mumbling about quitting the band.

Matters came to a head one night at a group meeting in the Byrds' kitchen. After arguing for a while, some of the band members got mad and stood up to leave. Before they got out the door, James Brown called them back. "How are we going to break up? We haven't done anything yet!" Brown said angrily. "We don't need to be talking about quitting. We need to be talking about working harder!"

He made a good point—the band was really just getting started. The guys came back, and from then on the meeting became a discussion about how the group could improve itself. One thing they talked about was changing their name. That night, the Toccoa Band became The Flames. The name was a good choice, because they were going to get hotter and hotter.

Please, Please, Please

As the Flames' popularity grew, they took on more gigs that were farther away. Their day jobs became a bigger hassle—for them as well as for their bosses! They started taking a lot of time off. When they did make it to work, they were often very tired. There were some days when James Brown came close to falling asleep on the job. Eventually he was fired for missing so much work. Before his parole officer could do anything about it, though, Brown had already found a job as a janitor at the Toccoa High School.

One day a friend made a suggestion that James Brown took to heart. "Why don't you write some of your own songs?" his friend asked. "After all, when the audience hollers, they're really hollering for the song itself." Brown knew this was good advice. He'd always had song ideas running through his mind. Now he started to pay a little more attention to those ideas. And when he finally got around to working on a song, he discovered that he had a natural talent for writing music.

His first song was called "Please, Please, Please." The very first time the Flames played it in public, the crowd loved it. The audience insisted that the group play it over and over again. The crowd's reaction gave Brown the confidence he needed to keep writing.

Around this time, Bobby Byrd was working at the Ritz as a janitor. The Ritz was Toccoa's movie house. It also booked bands. Like a lot of places then, it was segregated. "I don't know," the manager said nervously when Bobby asked him to book the Flames. "I don't want anything happening here." Bobby argued that lots of whites had heard the group, and they'd never had any trouble. Finally, the manager agreed to give them a chance. The show went off without a hitch, and the Flames became regulars at the Ritz.

Not everyone liked the Flames, however. Some of the church leaders in the community thought their music was sinful. They threatened to throw the young men out of their churches if they kept on playing "the devil's music." But some of the parents of the band members thought this idea was foolish. They protested to the church leaders and kept this from happening.

James Brown was relieved. Going to church was another condition of his parole. No matter how late he'd been up the night before, he—and the rest of the group, too—hardly ever missed a Sunday service.

After everyone had calmed down, the Flames made a trip to Atlanta, Georgia. They had been invited to appear on Piano Red's radio show on WAOK. They could hardly believe it. The days of their first awkward rehearsals in Bobby Byrd's living room now seemed far away. **These** days they were on big-city radio!

The Famous Flames

James Brown and the Flames had tasted success. Now they wanted more. Toccoa started to

Shown above are James Brown (on drums), Bobby Byrd (on piano), and the rest of the original Flames.

seem too small for them. If they wanted to get anywhere with their music, they decided, they would have to move to Macon, Georgia. Macon had a very active musical scene. The group wanted to get in on the action.

Making the move wasn't all that easy. For one thing, leaving Toccoa would violate Brown's parole. That problem was solved when Brown was assigned a new parole officer in Macon. A more difficult problem had to do with The Flames' manager, Barry Trimier. He owned a funeral home, and couldn't leave town. But he didn't want to hold them back, either. "Go ahead—and good luck," Barry told the group.

Short on cash and unsure of his musical future, James Brown moved to Macon. His family stayed behind in Toccoa, which was about a three-hour drive from his new home. Performing mainly on weekends, he managed to spend most of the week with Velma and their two young sons.

A man named Clint Brantly became the new manager of the Flames. One of the first changes he made was their name. "Since you aren't from around here, why don't we call you the Famous Flames?" he suggested. No one in the band objected to that! It was a big boost to their egos.

Brantly also managed a young rock 'n roll singer named Little Richard. At that time, Little Richard was very popular locally. He was still unknown outside of the Macon area, however. In fact, when he wasn't singing, he worked as a dishwasher at a bus station. Then his song "Tutti Frutti" soared to the top of the national charts. Without any explanation, Little Richard left for California in search of musical success.

Little Richard's sudden disappearance put Clint Brantly in a bind. What would happen to all the show dates that were already booked? It would be a disaster! Then he had an idea. He sent James Brown out in Little Richard's place, together with Richard's band and backup singers. Some of the people who attended these shows thought James Brown really was Little Richard! And nobody felt let down. James Brown might not have been as well known as Little Richard was at that point, but he had a magic all his own. Audiences loved him.

In the meantime, Bobby Byrd led the Famous Flames. Brown rejoined the group after he finished doing the shows for Little Richard. This situation got them all some good exposure.

The Famous Flames liked to hear what other groups were doing. Even better, they liked to "cut in" the groups, especially the more popular ones. When intermission came, the Famous Flames would sometimes jump up onstage and start playing. They'd get the audience so worked up that **they'd** be the ones finishing the show, not the original group! Before long, even the very best bands were afraid to let them onstage.

Many of these groups, such as the Drifters and the Midnighters, already had records out. James Brown decided that it was time for the Famous Flames to do the same thing. First, though, they had to make a demonstration tape to take to a record company. There was no question about what song to record. It would be "Please, Please, Please."

The demo was made at radio station WIBB. The station's owner liked them so much that he didn't even charge them for the use of the station's studio! The local record companies, however, didn't share his enthusiasm for the Famous Flames. "Sorry, not interested," was the reply most of the time.

In the meantime, a disk jockey on radio station WBML began to play the tape on the radio. It didn't take long before the request lines were ringing off the hook. "Where can I get the record?" people asked. "Play that song again!" They were disappointed when they discovered that a record didn't even exist.

Encouraged by this response, James Brown decided to try his luck at the Southland Record Distributing Company in Atlanta. There he gave his demo to a woman who used to work for King Records. When she listened to the song, she liked it so much that she played it for Ralph Bass, one of King's talent scouts. Bass, too, was impressed.

One rainy night in January 1956, the Famous Flames were playing in a club near Milledgeville, Georgia. While they were performing, they noticed a white man standing in a corner. This didn't surprise them at all. "He's probably another club owner, checking us out," Brown thought.

At intermission, the man came over to talk with them. "Like the show," he said. "Do you have many original songs?" Brown assured him they did, and started talking about a dance routine— thinking, of course, that a club owner would be interested in their stage act. But that's not what the man had in mind. "I want you to record for King Records," Ralph Bass told them.

James Brown's first big hit was "Please, Please, Please."
He next released "Try Me," which reached number one on
the R & B charts and even made it to the pop charts!

James Brown and the Famous Flames could put together a stage act that was hard to beat! This photo was taken around 1962.

Backstage at Harlem's Apollo Theater, James Brown flashes a smile. He's shown here with emcee Danny Ray.

"The Hardest Working Man in Show Business" dances up a storm.

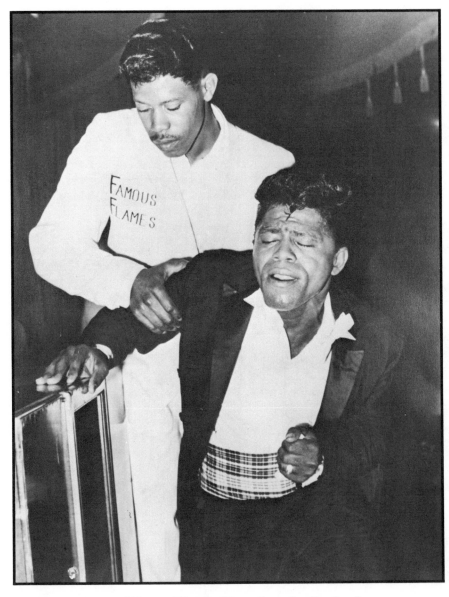

Having just sung "Please, Please, Please" as the finale of a 1962 performance, an exhausted James Brown falls to his knees.

4 CHAPTER | HITTING THE BIG TIME

"You didn't see too many groups like us, dancing all over the place, cutting flips, slinging sweat, and singing real raw."

—James Brown

Workin'
Up a Sweat

The Famous Flames signed a contract with King Records just one day after they first met Ralph Bass. Early the following month, when they were playing some clubs in Florida, they got the call they'd been waiting for. "King wants you in Cincinnati as soon as possible," their manager told them. "They want to record."

The group quickly drove to Macon, and then went on to Cincinnati. It was the first time any of them had been out of the South. Even though they'd been driving for hours, they were too excited to sleep. When they arrived, they went straight to King Records.

It took several days for their session to be set, however. Delay followed delay. They began to wonder if they'd ever do any recording. And when they finally did get in to record, they faced a new problem. Syd Nathan, the man who had started King Records, hated "Please, Please, Please." "Nobody wants to hear that noise!" he exclaimed grumpily. It looked like the Famous Flames' recording career would be finished before it even got started.

Luckily, Ralph Bass and others came to their defense. They did their best to convince Nathan to give the Famous Flames a chance. At last they succeeded, and Nathan allowed the session to go on. Besides "Please," the group recorded "Why Do You Do Me Like You Do," "I Feel that Old Feeling Coming On," and "I Don't Know." Despite the harsh criticism they'd just received, the group tried to sing with as much confidence and energy as ever. Then they headed for home, not knowing what would happen next.

Back in Macon, they heard some bad news. Syd Nathan hated all of their songs as much as he said he would. Not only that, but Ralph Bass had been fired. The Famous Flames were very worried. It didn't look like a record would ever be released!

Then, for some reason, Mr. Nathan changed his mind. "Please, Please, Please" was released as a single on the Federal division of King Records on March 3, 1956. The song wasn't too popular at first. Gradually, though, it caught on. It stayed on *Billboard's* R & B Chart for 19 weeks, and even reached the number six position. This was really a very good showing for a first record. Its success got Ralph Bass his old job back.

A lot of people were surprised that "Please" did as well as it did. James Brown and the Famous Flames were very different from what people were used to hearing. At that time, a lot of the R & B groups sang close harmony. Some of them even wore top hats and canes. Not the Famous Flames! They wore wild red suits, and weren't afraid to show their audiences that they were working hard. "You didn't see too many groups like us, dancing all over the place, cutting flips, slinging sweat, and singing real raw," Brown remembered. That rawness came through on their records, and appealed to lots of people.

The group went back to Cincinnati for more recording sessions in March and July of 1956. That summer and fall, many more singles were released. These included "I Don't Know," "Hold My Baby's Hand," and "Just Won't Do Right."

But James Brown wasn't all that happy with what was happening. With so many new songs out at the same time, people were getting confused. In a way, James Brown's records were competing with each other for sales.

Still, having records out got them better gigs. And although Brown was still subject to the conditions of his parole—which included staying away from Augusta—he managed to get permission to perform there. In Augusta he got to see his father, Aunt Minnie, Honey, and even Big Junior, who was visiting from New York. It was quite a happy reunion. They knew all about his records. "Isn't it incredible?" they took turns exclaiming. Honey was the only one who wasn't surprised. She had predicted something big for James Brown all along.

Changes Ahead

One night the Famous Flames were booked in Atlanta with several other acts, including Hank Ballard and the Midnighters. The show was to bring about a lot of important changes for the group. But no one could have guessed that from the way things started.

The group wasn't exactly sure when it was supposed to perform. A couple of the guys thought there was plenty of time before it was their turn to go on. They went out to get something to eat. Then the rest of the group discovered that they were the second act! The Famous Flames stalled as long as they could after the first act was finished. Finally, though, they had to go on—the crowd was getting anxious.

Just then, the two missing players came back and saw what was happening. As they threw on their stage costumes, James Brown did some quick thinking. Dancing a step called the "mashed potatoes" to the side of the stage, he brought on the band members one at a time. It looked as smooth as if they'd planned it all along! The audience got all worked up, and the Famous Flames went on to give a terrific show.

Hank Ballard, for one, was very impressed with the Famous Flames. He phoned Ben Bart, his booking agent at Universal Attractions in New York. "I think I've just seen an act Universal should sign," he said. It wasn't long before a deal was arranged. Ben Bart and James Brown would become business partners—and lifelong friends.

Early in 1957, Mr. Bart decided to call the group James Brown and the Famous Flames. After all, Brown had been the lead performer all along. Now it was time to really develop his star potential.

This news didn't set too well with the rest of the group, however. Ever since that first big quarrel when they were just starting out, jealousy had been a big problem. Changing the act's name was the final straw. The band was not able to work things out. Except for James Brown, everybody decided to call it quits.

Brown was terribly disappointed, but he wasn't about to let the group's decision slow him down. After the breakup, he hired other musicians and began performing in Florida. "That's what you do—you just keep working," James Brown commented later. "It's just like I do now."

When Little Richard suddenly retired from rock 'n' roll in October 1957, James Brown was again asked to make up some of Richard's broken dates. This time everyone could tell the two singers apart! There was also a side benefit to this arrangement. When the tour was over, Brown put together a new group from Little Richard's band. James Brown and the Famous Flames were back.

Even as Brown's professional life soared, his home life started to come apart. By now James Brown and Velma had a third son. But with all the work that was going into his career, Brown couldn't get home as often as he used to. This meant that Velma was pretty much raising the children by herself. When he did make it back, he and Velma had little to say to each other. Eventually they were divorced, although they remained friends.

Apollo Action

As well as things were going in the career of James Brown, there was still a big problem. Except for "Please, Please, Please," none of his other records had done all that well. He needed to record some more hits. Syd Nathan at King Records wasn't very encouraging. He wanted to drop James Brown. "James Brown is a has-been," he told people.

Brown was never one to back down easily, however. For some time, he'd been playing a song he had written called "Try Me," which the audiences loved. Their reaction told Brown that he had another hit on his hands—that is, if he could ever get Mr. Nathan to record it!

Using his own money, he paid to have a demo of the song made. Then he had some copies made in acetate, and distributed them to all the disk jockeys he knew. From Macon to Nashville, "Try Me" became one of the most-requested songs at radio stations. When Nathan found out that there were already orders for 22,000 copies of the record, he could hardly refuse to put it out.

"Try Me" was recut in September 1958 and released the next month. The song quickly reached the number one spot on the R & B charts. It even went to number 48 on the pop charts! This was unusual success for a rhythm and blues song. James Brown had proved once again that he knew what he was doing.

Brown was a very disciplined performer, both in the recording studio and in live concerts. He wanted his group to be the same way, and could be rather demanding. Some of the back-up singers resented this. After a tense fight in Oakland, California, the second set of Famous Flames quit. Once again Brown was without a band.

The timing of this big change couldn't have been worse. When Brown got back to Macon, he found out that he'd been booked at the Apollo Theater in New York. The Apollo hosted some of the best performers in black show business. Apollo audiences were tough. The shows—sometimes six or seven performances a day—were grueling. Succeeding at the Apollo meant that a performer had succeeded, period.

Although James Brown had just two weeks to get ready, he decided to go ahead with the engagement. "You take your opportunities when they come," he said. Former Flame Johnny Terry, who had been in and out of the group for several years, agreed to work with him. So did Baby Lloyd Stallworth and Bobby Bennet. They went to New York and started rehearsing—hard.

Two days before the first show, Bobby Byrd showed up. Byrd and Brown had stayed friends through all that had happened. Now Byrd was glad to be a part of this important event. "Let's get to it," said Bobby.

James Brown and the Famous Flames performed at the Apollo for the first time the week of April 24, 1959. When they started, they were at the bottom of the billing. The star of the show was Little Willie John. But by the end of the week, James Brown and the Famous Flames were co-starring. The tough Apollo audience was crazy for them!

James Brown was the talk of the town. And one person, in particular, paid close attention to what was said.

After the Apollo engagement was over, Brown was getting ready to leave his hotel when he heard a knock at the door. Standing in the doorway was a small, middle-aged woman. Brown recognized her right away. "I've been looking for you for a long time," he said, and hugged her. It was the first time he'd seen his mother in over 20 years.

Susie Brown was living in Brooklyn. From then on, whenever James Brown had a date at the Apollo, he would get in touch with his mother. They spent a lot of time talking, and gradually became close. But Brown never went into details about the house on Twiggs Street, or about his time in prison. He didn't want to make his mother feel bad.

5 CHAPTER

DOING
SOME
GOOD

"It was about the roots of black music, and it was kind of a pride thing, too, being proud of yourself and your people."

—James Brown discussing soul music

A Hit Album

By now, James Brown was performing nearly 350 nights a year. In a normal month, he was on stage for 80 hours—singing and dancing up such a sweat that he usually lost around seven pounds a night! He definitely deserved his new nickname, "The Hardest Working Man in Show Business."

James Brown wanted to last in the music business. With only a seventh-grade education, he feared that there was nothing else he could do. That's why he kept up such a frantic pace. And that's why he placed so much importance on discipline. As his shows kept adding people, this became even more essential.

To keep his shows running smoothly, he even set up a fining system. Band members had to pay a certain amount if they were late for rehearsals or shows. They also had to pay fines if they had a dirty uniform or scuffed-up shoes. They weren't the only ones who had to pay, though. If James Brown was guilty of any of these errors, he fined himself! The money went into a fund to pay for parties for the whole group.

Whenever he had the chance, he recorded new songs for release. The recording sessions went smoothly most of the time. Because the songs had already been played so many times, there was no need for the band to refine them. Brown already had a pretty good idea of what the people liked, and of what worked and what didn't.

For a long time, James Brown had been dancing the mashed potatoes in his act. He thought that a special piece of music for the dance would be a big hit. Mr. Nathan at King Records didn't agree. But Brown went ahead and cut the piece anyway, at Dade Records. Then he had a DJ dub his voice over his own, so he wouldn't break his contract with King. "(Do The) Mashed Potatoes, Parts 1 and 2" was released in February 1960. It made the R & B top 10. Once again, Brown's instincts about what people liked were right.

Even James Brown couldn't have guessed how much some people would like the song, however. One night James Brown was late to a performance. When he got to the club, the band was playing the instrumental "Mashed Potatoes." Brown was confused. Usually the band opened with that number, and by this time they should have been way past opening. He soon found out the reason for this mystery. A man sitting at the front table was flashing a gun at the group to make them keep playing the song! Finally, after five or six times through the song, the man slowly stood up. "Sure do like that tune," he said, and wandered off.

Before long James Brown had plans for another trend-setting project. He wanted to record a live album at the Apollo, and let people hear what kind of show he had. But Syd Nathan thought it was just too risky. Live albums weren't very common then. The project would cost a lot of money, and the album might not sell well.

But Brown wasn't about to give up. "All right then," he said. "I'll pay for the recording myself." The session was set for a Wednesday night. This was "amateur night" at the Apollo, and the crowds were usually more wild then. This time was no exception. By the time it was Brown's turn to perform, the audience was very turned on. There was even a little old lady in the front row who was so excited, she couldn't keep from swearing! Luckily her words were hard to understand. If they **hadn't** been, the album couldn't have been played on the radio.

King Records finally agreed to give the album a try. They bought the tape from Brown, and released the first *Live at the Apollo* album in January 1963. No one—not even James Brown—could have predicted what would happen next.

At that time, the music industry placed most of its emphasis on hit singles. Hit albums were rare. The plan for James Brown's new record was to see which songs from the album the radio stations were playing most. Then those songs would be released as singles. But as it turned out, many of the stations were playing the entire album! The record was on the charts for 66 weeks. It even reached the number two position.

Changing Policy

The enormous success of *Live at the Apollo* meant that James Brown's audience was changing. Until then, just about all of his fans were black. Now, however, a lot of white people were buying his music—even though it wasn't played very often on the white radio stations. This type of interest was still rare in the early 1960's.

Unfortunately, that attitude didn't always extend to live performances. Many auditoriums and concert halls still had policies of segregation. James Brown tried to change those policies whenever possible. In *Godfather of Soul*, he recalled a performance he once gave in a ballpark. "During the show the white kids started coming down toward the stage," Brown says. "Before long there were white kids and black kids crowding around the stage, dancing and hollering and having a good time. They had integrated themselves."

James Brown took a firm stand on this issue when he performed in Macon. After all, Macon was like his second hometown. "If the concert is segregated," he said, "I won't go on." The city officials decided to give it a try, and the concert went off without incident. Everyone—black and white— had a great time.

Several months later, Brown did the same thing in Augusta. There he gave the first integrated event in the history of Bell Auditorium. To a person who'd grown up with water fountains labeled "white drinking water" and "colored drinking water," this was a treasured accomplishment.

Shortly after that concert, President Lyndon B. Johnson signed the 1964 Civil Rights Bill. The bill made segregation in public places illegal. It also dealt with school integration, fair employment practices, and voter registration.

Papa's New Bag

1964 also marked a change of direction for Brown. In that year, James Brown released a new song called "Out of Sight." In it, the instruments and voices were used to create simple rhythmic accents. The new rhythms were easily heard, and the people loved it. "Out of Sight" rocketed to the top of the R & B charts.

The new song was released on the Mercury/ Smash label instead of King. This put James Brown in the midst of a legal tug-of-war between the two record companies. The courts finally decided that he could sing only on King, and play only instrumentals on Mercury. The court decision didn't have anything to do with his live performances, though. James Brown went right on making his audiences feel good.

By now, James Brown had become a cultural hero. He made appearances on television shows such as "The Ed Sullivan Show" and "Where the Action Is." He even became a regular on Dick Clark's "American Bandstand."

One of the most telling signs of his success came with his performance in 1965 on the "T.A.M.I. Show." This television program featured lots of popular musical acts. It was an enormous hit with the teenagers of that time.

While taping the program in November 1964,

James Brown met the Rolling Stones for the first time. They were really big then, and were the featured act of the show. Even so, they were nervous about following James Brown. He was **hot** that day, and the audience knew it. They kept calling him back for encores. "I don't think they'd ever seen a man move that fast!" Brown said of his dancing. Behind the scenes, Mick Jagger of the Stones was watching carefully. From then on, it seemed, he put more energy into his stage moves.

In 1965, James Brown got a better deal with King Records. Besides getting higher royalties, he was given more creative power, too. Shortly after reaching the new agreement, he put out a song on King called "Papa's Got a Brand New Bag." In this sense, the word "bag" means a concept or idea. In the song, Brown expanded on the changes he'd started with "Out of Sight."

The new song's title was quite descriptive, for James Brown had created a type of music called funk. In 1988, *Rolling Stone* included "Papa's Got a Brand New Bag" in its list of Top 100 Singles of the Past 25 Years. "With this song, James Brown revolutionized dance music," the magazine reported. "He turned R & B into a whole new bag; he invented funk."

Americans were not the only people excited about James Brown. People in England, especially, were enthusiastic about his music. In early 1966 he went there to tape a television show called "Ready Steady Go." Some of the most popular British acts—including the Beatles, the Kinks, and the Animals—came by just to meet him.

No matter where James Brown was when he gave a concert, he continued to live up to his reputation as "The Hardest-Working Man in Show Business." In fact, sometimes he worked **too** hard. One night, at the end of an Apollo performance, he collapsed. Some of the fans could tell that this wasn't just part of his act. They started screaming while the Flames carried Brown backstage.

A doctor diagnosed Brown's problem as low-salt syndrome, caused by sweating out too much sodium and potassium. He gave James Brown an intravenous solution (IV) to correct the imbalance. After that, whenever Brown started feeling too exhausted, he took an IV. Some people saw the needle mark in his arm and started saying he was a junkie.

Another rumor made the rounds, too. "Did you hear the news?" people said under their breaths. "James Brown is having a sex-change operation so he can marry Bobby Byrd!" But Brown and Byrd laughed it off. They knew that this outrageous rumor had been started by none other than Brown's own manager, Ben Bart. It was just a ploy to create some excitement and have a little fun with the press—and it worked!

Don't Be a Drop-out

To keep up with the demands of his music career, James Brown decided to lease his own full-time jet. It was a six-passenger Lear jet, painted white and green with the words "Out of Sight" written on its sides. Having the jet meant he could work more—and rest more, too. And besides that, the jet was an impressive symbol of his success.

Yet James Brown wanted to do more with his fame than just gather up expensive possessions. He wanted to make a difference in the world. One issue he felt strongly about was education. With the release of his song "Don't Be A Drop-out" in 1966, James Brown started a national campaign to encourage kids to graduate from high school. He worked closely with Vice President Hubert Humphrey, and even presented the vice president with the first copy of his new song.

In between shows, James Brown went from school to school, talking with the kids. He told them to pay attention to their studies and stick it out. "If I hadn't been blessed with musical ability," he admitted to them, "I'd still be a janitor." He also sent out a newsletter, and started "Don't Be A Drop-out" clubs.

For about six months, he even gave away $500 scholarships to black colleges as part of his shows. Not all of the winners really listened to his message, though, which was very frustrating for Brown. "This one kid said, 'Hey, James, who don't you just give me $500 in cash, man, so I can buy some sharp clothes and be hip like you,'" he wrote in *Godfather of Soul*. "I didn't know whether to cry or hit the kid. Some of them just didn't understand, and it broke my heart to see it."

A Troubled Nation

By now the Civil Rights Bill had been in effect for two years. But although the law had changed, many of the old attitudes remained. There was still a lot of anger and resentment between blacks and whites. James Brown was very concerned about this. Hoping to make a positive statement, he joined the National Association for the Advancement of Colored People (NAACP).

The summer of 1967 brought the problem of race relations to the foreground. Riots broke out all over the country. In Newark, New Jersey, 26 people were killed. In Detroit, Michigan, the death toll was 43. Thousands of people were hurt. Houses were burned, and businesses were destroyed.

It was during this turbulent time that James

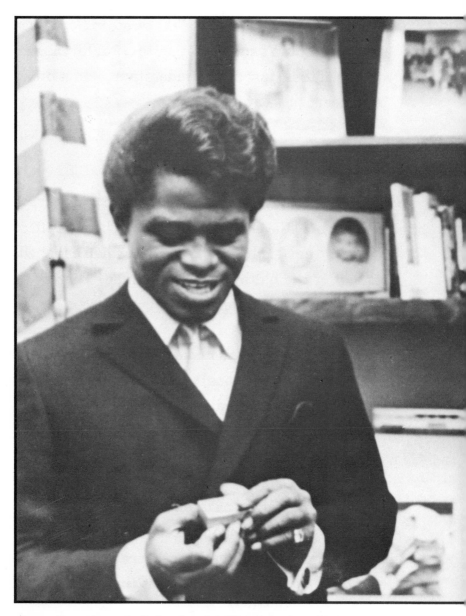

James Brown worked closely with Vice President Hubert Humphrey during Brown's "Don't Be A Drop-out" campaign, which began in 1966.

Brown got the name Soul Brother Number One. By now, the word "soul" had taken on some new meanings. As James Brown has explained, "It was about the roots of black music, and it was kind of a pride thing, too, being proud of yourself and your people."

James Brown found a new way to express some of that pride when he bought several radio stations, including WRDW in Augusta. His stations featured soul, gospel, and jazz, along with talk shows that discussed the concerns of the black community. At that time, there were over 500 black-oriented radio stations in the United States. But only five of those were actually owned by blacks—and three of those were owned by James Brown!

James Brown didn't buy the stations to make money. But he did want to be a symbol of the black business owner, in the hope that other blacks would follow his example. He believed that black ownership was a peaceful way to obtain power.

The country was still far from peaceful, however. A lot of people were upset about the Vietnam

War. They didn't think the United States should be involved in the conflict, and protests were held all across the country. Then, in April 1968, the non-violent civil rights leader, Martin Luther King, Jr., was assassinated. Riots broke out once more.

James Brown did all he could to prevent that kind of violence. In Boston the day after the shooting, he gave the televised concert referred to at the beginning of this book. The show helped calm people and kept them off the streets. The next day he made several radio and television appeals in Washington, D.C. "The real answer to race problems in this country is education. Not burning and killing," he told the audiences. "Be ready. Be qualified. Own something. Be somebody," he added. "That's Black Power."

Brown's efforts didn't go unnoticed. On May 8, 1968, President Lyndon B. Johnson invited James Brown to a state dinner at the White House. His place card read, "Thanks much for what you are doing for your country.—LBJ."

Less than a month later, James Brown went off to entertain the troops in Vietnam. He and the seven people he was allowed to take with him stayed at the Continental Hotel in Saigon. Danger was everywhere. The day they arrived, a mortar shell exploded down the block and killed 17 people. That morning, 10 rockets were dropped on the air base outside the city. James Brown performed at the air base that same afternoon.

Brown and his group performed two or three shows a day. A helicopter took them from place to place, and returned them to their hotel in Saigon to sleep. Doing the shows took a lot of energy. Most of the time it was around 100 degrees. Brown never complained, though. He knew that for the troops, listening to James Brown's music gave a much-needed lift.

Backlash!

When entertainers become involved in politics, they often upset their fans who don't agree with them. This started happening to James Brown. Before he went to Vietnam, James Brown had released a song called "America is My Home."

When he came back, he discovered that a lot of black people were very angry about the song. "How can you sing that after what happened to Dr. King?" they asked. James Brown tried to explain that he was celebrating the American land and its people, not the government. Not everyone got the message, though.

To top that off, other black fans were upset because he had a white bass player in his group. James Brown stood firm on that issue. If he thought a person was talented and sincere, what did it matter what color his or her skin was? To James Brown, music was music. Everybody had a right to it.

That same summer, James Brown went to Watts—a black district in Los Angeles—and campaigned for Hubert Humphrey for president. All of his political activities had his manager, Ben Bart, wringing his hands. Bart tried to slow him down. But James Brown just replied, "It would be a shame to have this big audience and not try to do some good."

Before 1968 was over, Brown released a song

that was just as controversial as "America is My Home"—but for the opposite reason. The new one was called "Say It Loud, I'm Black and I'm Proud." This song cost him many of his white fans. They thought James Brown sounded militant and anti-white. In spite of their reaction, "I'm Black and I'm Proud" made it to the number one spot on the R & B charts. It even made it to number 10 on the pop charts.

Brown's involvement in politics continued to draw attention. January 1969 marked the beginning of a new presidential administration. Even though Brown had campaigned for Hubert Humphrey, President Nixon invited him to sing at the inaugural gala, along with some other groups. Brown sang two songs, including "I'm Black and I'm Proud." But the fact that he performed at all drew more protests from the black community.

By now James Brown was getting tired of being misunderstood. He started working on a new song that he hoped would set matters straight. "I Don't Want Nobody to Give Me Nothing" was released in March. The title and lyrics of the song explained

James Brown's position on the race issue. "I wanted to let the black people know that nobody **owed** you anything for being an Afro-American. And I wanted to let the white people know that all anybody wants is a fair chance," Brown later explained.

Despite all the controversy, James Brown was still one of the most effective black leaders of the time. Two years after he'd helped calm the race riots in 1968, he was needed to do the same thing—this time in his hometown.

It all started when a 16-year-old black boy was beaten to death in the Richmond County Jail. This was the same jail in which James Brown himself had turned 16. The sheriff said that the boy's cellmates were the ones who were responsible for the death. But a lot of black people were saying that the prison guards—who were white—were to blame. At first the protests were peaceful, though the tension was mounting. When a student set fire to the Georgia state flag, riots exploded.

James Brown had been playing a gig in Michigan. As soon as he heard the news, he flew back to do what he could to calm people down. He went directly to the jail and held a press conference there. Then he went to his radio station. Together with Bobby Byrd, he broadcasted appeals—live and taped—around the clock. The two performers even went out into the streets with the station's remote unit. Although some people were too angry to listen to them, many got the message and went home.

6 CHAPTER READY TO WALK THE LINE

"*Unless you do puzzles, you cannot hope to understand James Brown.*"

—**James Brown**

"Taking Some Mess"

The 1970's brought a lot of changes into the life of James Brown. By now his divorce from Velma was final. He married his second wife, Deidre, on October 22, 1970. The ceremony was performed in a judge's home near Barnwell, South Carolina. That was just a few miles from the cabin in the woods where he was born.

Other changes had a more negative impact on his life. When James Brown supported the re-election of President Nixon in 1972, many fans thought he'd gone one step too far. James Brown—Soul Brother Number One—was actually picketed in Baltimore and elsewhere. Hecklers sometimes disrupted his shows. Attendance dropped.

James Brown defended his position. "I'm trying to put pressure on the government not to forget about us, " he explained. "I'm trying to do some good." Few people understood his point.

The following years just got worse. His oldest son, Teddy, was killed in a car accident in the summer of 1973. The Internal Revenue Service claimed he owed millions of dollars in back taxes. His jet—which cost $550 per hour to run—had major mechanical problems and was repossessed. His radio stations were failing. So were the soul-food restaurants he'd started. In James Brown's words, "I took some mess."

Musically, the times were rough for James Brown, too. Both Ben Bart and Syd Nathan had died, and James Brown had signed with Polydor Records. Disco, considered an offshoot of funk, was getting very popular then. But to James Brown—and many music critics—disco was shallow, surface music.

Real funk went deeper, they thought. It was more complex and more human. Brown wanted to keep on putting out hard funk records. His recording company thought differently. Polydor wanted him to tone down his style in order to appeal to a new audience.

Also upsetting to James Brown was the death of Elvis Presley in August 1977. Brown had spent time with Elvis and had considered him a friend.

In many ways, they were a lot alike. They were both poor boys from the South, who grew up listening to gospel and rhythm and blues. They both made it big in the same year, Elvis with "Hound Dog" and Brown with "Please Please Please." Brown had a hard time accepting the fact that Elvis was gone. "You rat," he muttered over Elvis' open coffin. Tears were in his eyes. "Why'd you leave me? How could you let it go?"

On Valentine's Day the next year, Brown suffered another loss. His second wife left him, taking with her their two young daughters. James Brown would miss them terribly.

Living in America

Despite the problems in his personal life, James Brown was a performer through and through. He started increasing his performance dates again. All the while, though, he made sure people knew one thing—James Brown was no "golden oldies" performer. He was a contemporary artist.

Other performers had a great deal of respect for him. In fact, some of today's biggest musical stars grew up watching and listening to James Brown. Once he was doing a show at the Beverly Theater in Los Angeles. Suddenly Prince and Michael Jackson jumped onstage and joined in the music. Needless to say, the crowd was thrilled!

Always up for new challenges, James Brown even tried his hand at acting. In 1980 he played a gospel-singing preacher in *Blues Brothers*, a hit movie with Dan Aykroyd and John Belushi. People in the younger generation—many of whom hadn't even heard of James Brown—became fans. Later he appeared in *Dr. Detroit*, again with Dan Aykroyd. By this time, John Belushi was dead from a drug overdose.

While taping a "Solid Gold" television show in 1982, James Brown met a hairstylist and makeup artist named Adrienne "Alphie" Rodriguez. Because she was in show business herself, she understood the life of an entertainer. She and Brown became very close, and were married in 1984.

Even during the slow periods of his career, no

one could deny James Brown's importance to the musical world. When things started happening for him again in 1986, his many fans were delighted. Brown's single, "Living in America," won him his first Grammy. And once more, he experienced the thrill of a platinum record with the soundtrack for *Rocky IV*.

The timing couldn't have been better. The soundtrack went to the top of the charts the very same night that James Brown was inducted into the Rock and Roll Hall of Fame. Although Brown didn't sing rock music, he was honored to be inducted with such people as Buddy Holly, Elvis Presley, Chuck Berry, Little Richard, and Fats Domino. "I think I felt for the first time that the struggle was over," he said.

Out of Touch

"Unless you do puzzles," James Brown once said, "you cannot hope to understand James Brown." By the late 1980's, even his family and friends had to agree with that statement. The

Godfather of Soul was making news once more—but this time, it was because of his conflicts with the law.

In late 1988, James Brown's attorney and agent confirmed the suspicion that the soul singer had a drug problem. The drug was PCP, or "angel dust." This is a very addictive hallucinogen. It causes people to distort reality and see things that aren't really there. The drug can make people think that others are "out to get them." Or it can convince them that no matter what they do, they won't be hurt.

"I never thought I'd see the day I'd be pleading with Mr. Brown about drugs," said one of Brown's close friends in an interview with *Rolling Stone*. Others agreed, remembering the days when he fined band members for taking a drink before a show. "Right now he's not James Brown," said his former tour manager. "He's a possessed James Brown."

For 10 years, Brown had used PCP very rarely. Eventually, though, it turned into a dangerous habit. His friends think it was the drug's effect on his personality that got him into trouble with the law.

And in 1988 there was plenty of trouble. He was arrested for domestic violence, but Adrienne Brown later dropped the charges. In a May incident, he was charged with possession of PCP, carrying a pistol, and resisting arrest. As part of his probation, he organized a poorly attended concert and wrestling benefit show.

In September he was involved in a high-speed car chase with police. This incident started in an Augusta office building he owns. In a rage about strangers using his private bathroom, he burst into an insurance seminar, waving two guns around. By the time police caught up with him, the chase involved more than 10 vehicles and had crossed into South Carolina. At one point, Brown even tried to run over two officers at a roadblock.

On December 15, 1988, James Brown was sentenced to six years in prison for failing to stop for police. He was given an option of fines or prison for two assault charges. He couldn't afford the fines, so he had to go to prison. James Brown couldn't escape spending time behind bars once again.

Perhaps, as many of his friends are hoping, the prison sentence will give Brown the time he needs to get back in touch with himself. "As far as I can tell, he's been straight," one of them said. "I think James Brown is ready to walk the line."

Bringing People Together

No matter how James Brown gets into the news, his music keeps on making people feel good. That was clear to see at the 1988 New Orleans Jazz Festival, where he was one of the main attractions. And when he gave a concert in East Berlin late that summer, he was met by 150,000 screaming German fans.

James Brown will always be remembered for his contribution to soul music—as well as to funk, R & B, and rap. Even when other black singers were "going commercial," James Brown bucked the trend and made it work for him. He put all his enormous energy into making his kind of music. He never stopped telling the people "James Brown, James Brown." In years to come, they will still be listening to that voice.

Yet the King of Soul—born into poverty, serving time by the age of 16, never getting beyond seventh grade—defines his success more simply. "Honors and gold records and all that aren't what I'm proudest of," James Brown once said. "I'm proudest of what I have become, as opposed to what I could have become. And I'd like to be remembered as someone who brought people together."

James Brown will always be remembered for his influence on soul, funk, rhythm and blues, and rap.

GLOSSARY

acetate—a demonstration record.

bail—money given as a pledge that a person will return for a court appearance.

civil rights—the rights of citizens guaranteed by the U.S.Constitution and by acts of Congress. This phrase often refers to the struggle of blacks and other minorities to be treated fairly under the law.

controversial—causing quarrels or strife between two opposing groups.

cut—to make a record.

demo—a "demonstration tape" of a song.

disco—dance music that has very catchy rhythms, simple lyrics and electronically produced sounds.

discrimination—to be treated unfairly due to prejudice.

emcee—a person who acts as a master of ceremonies.

encore—a demand by an audience for a repeat of a work.

funk—popular black music that is earthy and very easy to dance to.

gig—to work as a musician; a specific job.

gospel—a type of religious music.

hallucinogen—a substance that causes people to "see" things that aren't actually there.

harmony—music that compliments the melody, or main tune.

inaugural—having to do with the swearing in of a new president.

inducted—to be formally admitted as a member of an organization.

GLOSSARY

integrated—the bringing together of different racial groups; opposite of segregated.

intermission—a short break between the different parts of a performance.

IV—short for intravenous, or entering the body directly through the veins.

jazz—American music that uses rhythmic variations, improvisation and complicated melodies.

militant—aggressive; wanting to fight.

moonshine—corn whiskey that is made illegally.

parole—the conditions under which a prisoner may be released early from a sentence.

PCP—the drug phencyclidine, which affects the body's central nervous system.

quartet—a four-part musical composition or group.

R & B—short for rhythm & blues.

rap—a musical style that uses accented talking.

remote—broadcasting radio or television from a place other than the actual station.

rhythm & blues—black American vocal music, usually used for dancing.

royalties—payment made to an artist for each copy of the work sold.

segregation—separation of people based on race; opposite of integration.

soundtrack—the music that goes with a movie.

stamina—strength or endurance.

turbulent—a time of restlessness or disturbance.

INDEX

LISTENING CHOICES

Songs	Albums
"America Is My Home"	*Ain't It Funky*
"Bewildered"	*The Amazing James Brown*
"Cold Sweat"	*Cold Sweat*
"Don't Be A Drop-Out"	*Get Up Offa That Thing*
"Good Good Lovin'"	*Grits and Soul*
"I Don't Know"	*I Got You (I Feel Good)*
"I Got a Bag of My Own"	*It's a Man's Man's Man's*
"If I Ruled the World"	*World*
"Licking Stick"	*The James Brown Show*
"Living in America"	*JB and His Famous Flames*
"Mashed Potatoes"	*Tour the U.S.A.*
"Night Train"	*Live at the Apollo*
"Out of Sight"	*Live at the Garden*
"Papa's Got a Brand New Bag"	*Please Please Please*
	Raw Soul
"Please Please Please"	*Say It Loud, I'm Black &*
"Prisoner of Love"	*I'm Proud*
"Talkin' Loud and Sayin' Nothing"	*Sex Machine Live*
	Soul Classics
"Think"	*Soul Syndrome*
"Try Me"	*Think*
"Say It Loud, I'm Black & I'm Proud"	*Thinking About Little Willie John & a Few Nice Things*
"Sex Machine"	
"Why Do You Do Me"	*Try Me*